Baby ABC

Text copyright © 2024
Illustration copyright © 2024

All rights reserved. No part of this publication may be reproduced or transmitted in any form or by any means, electronic or mechanical, including photocopying, recording or by any information storage and retrieval system now known or to be invented, without permission in writing from the publisher.

Layout and design by Seong min Yoo
ISBN 978-1-7383320-0-7

Beaver Can Press fuels creativity and continues to publish books for every reader. Thank you for buying an authorized edition of this book. The artwork in this book was rendered in pen and digitally altered.

Written and illustrated by Seong min Yoo

Baby ABC

Baby

Bee

C

Chicken

Cat

Dragonfly

Dog

Eggplant

Elderberry

E

F

Fish

Frog

Goat

G

Grass

Hedgehog

Heart

H

Jaguar

Jeep

K

Kite

Kangaroo

L

Leaf

Lion

Moon

Mountain

M

N

Nightingale

Narwhal

Penguin

Polar bear

P

Q

Queen

Quartz

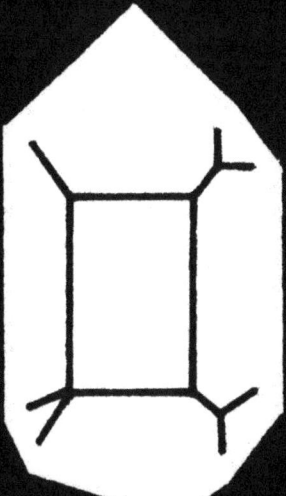

T Tree

Tiger

Volcano

V

Vulture

Wind

Wave

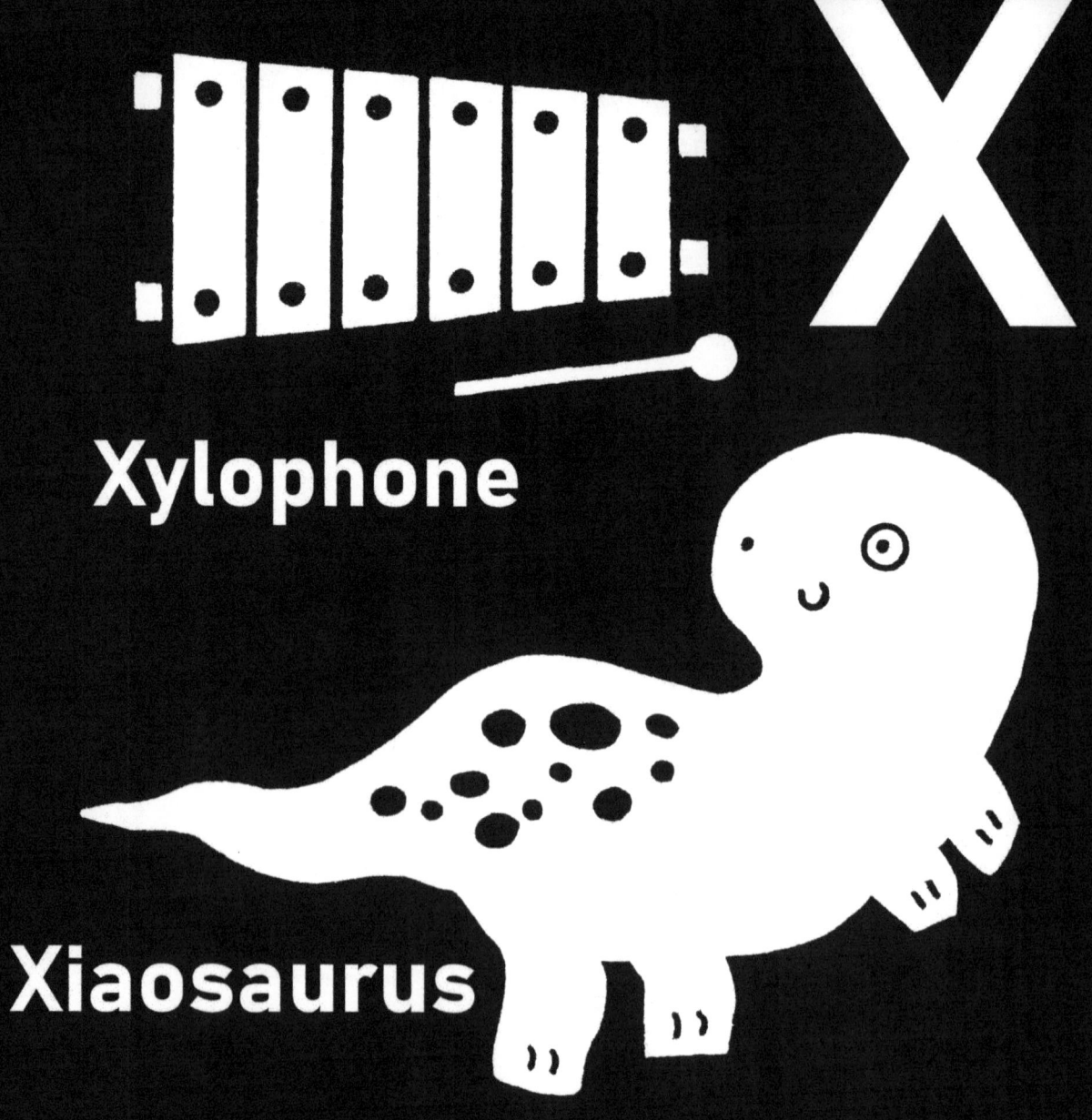

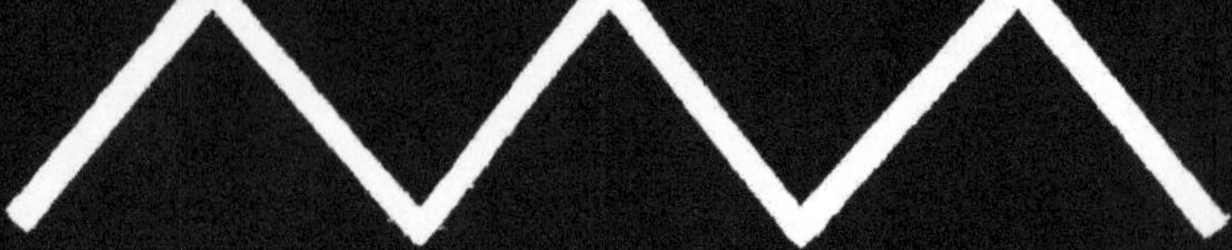

Zigzag

Z

Zebra

www.ingramcontent.com/pod-product-compliance
Lightning Source LLC
Chambersburg PA
CBHW042355070526
44585CB00028B/2944